THE GOLDEN YEARS

1957

text: David Sandison

design: Paul Kurzeja

SIENA

195

I f any one word sums up 1957, it's probably.....travel! Well, just look at a few of the events you'll find inside this look at the way we were in 1957, and you'll see the connection. Space travel became a reality this year, when the Russians stole a formidable lead on the United States. Not content with putting Sputnik-1 into orbit months ahead of America's much-delayed inaugural satellite launch, they had the nerve to put Laika, a cross-bred (and very photogenic) husky into orbit. If they could do it with a dog, how soon before they succeeded with a man?

Faced with the stubborn resistance of Arkansas State Governor Faubus, President Eisenhower gave travel orders to 1,500 National Guardsmen, who flew into Little Rock to make sure black students could enter the capital's Central High School, to join the white classmates United States law decreed they had the right to study alongside.

Sir Anthony Eden flew back from an enforced rest-break in the Bahamas to face the sack as Britain's Prime Minister, his punishment for leading the UK into the Suez Canal débâcle. Into his place stepped SuperMac, the name given to Harold Macmillan as he began to stamp his mark on history.

Delegates from six European countries travelled to Rome, where they signed a treaty which would create a Common Market organisation aimed, eventually, at

rivalling the trading and political strength of the US, the Soviet Bloc and the fast-rising Japanese.

Rock 'n' roll pioneer hit-maker Bill Haley travelled to Britain to show local teenagers what this new music was all about. There were huge crowds, headlines - and BBC Television elders sniffingly gave permission for the country's first weekly live pop show. The travel link? It was called 6.5 Special, and it featured an opening credits sequence of an express train.

Lastly, you'll find news of a new, unspoiled Spanish fishing village travel writers reckoned was the new up and coming holiday destination for those in the know. It's name? Benidorm.

Macmillan Replaces Disgraced Eden As Prime Minister

HAROLD MACMILLAN became Britain's new Prime Minister today, taking on the task of rebuilding the country's international credibility - and mending Anglo-US relations - from Sir Anthony Eden, who resigned two days ago on the grounds of ill-health.

No-one was fooled by the reasons given for Eden's departure. While doctors had forced the 59 year old PM to take a three-week 'rest cure' in November, the truth is that his decision to involve Britain in the disastrous Anglo-French invasion of the Suez Canal Zone last October - a move which met with immediate UN condemnation and the rare sight of US and Soviet delegates voting together - had destroyed his ability to represent the UK.

Many had expected RAB Butler, who'd served as acting prime minister during Eden's absence, to succeed him. But, behind the scenes, Conservative Party whips learned that there would have been a back-bench revolt if Butler got the job. The Queen met with Tory elders Sir Winston Churchill and the Marquess of Salisbury before asking Macmillan to take over.

It's clear that Butler's dogged support of Eden's conduct during Suez had tarred him with the same brush. On the other hand, Macmillan - the Chancellor of the Exchequer who'd heard US Treasury threats not to defend sterling against the international money market run which Suez sparked unless Britain pulled its troops out - had become an early pragmatic dove.

Macmillan dismissed Labour Party leader Hugh Gaitskell's call for a general election and busied himself with the huge task ahead, a fence-mending summit with the recently re-elected President Eisenhower his first priority (pictured right).

A bitterly disappointed RAB Butler received the consolation prize of becoming Home Secretary in Macmillan's first cabinet, with Peter Thorneycroft replacing the new PM as Chancellor.

UK Forces Drive Yemenis From Aden

Men of the Durham Light Infantry were at the heart of battle today when a combined force of troops and RAF fighters beat off an attack by Yemeni forces in the British protectorate of Aden at the southern entrance to the Red Sea. Aden, a military stronghold and naval fuelling station which has given Britain strategic access to the Arab region, the Suez Canal and the Indian Ocean since its annexation in 1839, is situated on a peninsula in the heart of territory 'borrowed' from what are now the modern states of Yemen and Saudi Arabia. The Yemenis now want it back.

Today's engagement saw Yemeni raiders driven from villages they'd over-run just inside the Aden border by a combination of ground mortars and airborne rocket and cannon fire.

JANUARY 4

UN Teams Begin To Clear Suez Canal

A United Nations-sponsored team of German tugs and salvage vessels began to clear a passage through the Suez Canal today, allowing 13 international ships stranded among the wreckage of the recent conflict to start negotiating their way north to the Mediterranean entrance at Port Said. Some of the debris was created by Egyptian engineers at the height of the three-pronged attacks launched initially by the Israelis, who seized the disputed Gaza Strip territory and the Sinai Peninsula region, and Anglo-French forces whose invasion was said to be a response to that action and aimed at ensuring the integrity of the Canal.

The UN team managed to shift a 350-ton tower from a collapsed railway bridge to widen the narrow channel and enable British and French vessels to begin work at clearing 12 sunken ships and restore the channel to its full width. Britain knows that, even when the Canal is restored to full working order, it will no longer be allowed access in wartime. On January 1, Egyptian President Colonel Gamal Nasser announced his country was tearing up the 1954 treaty which gave the UK guaranteed use of the strategic waterway during international conflicts.

JANUARY 10

Ike Swears To Continue Anti-Red Fight

In Washington today, President Eisenhower used the inaguration ceremony which officially confirmed his overwhelming defeat of Democrat challenger Adlai Stevenson last November, to dedicate his second term in office to a continued US vigilance against the spread of Communism and support for those countries fighting off the attacks of Soviet and Chinese sponsored insurgents.

Citing Russia's invasion of Hungary in November, when Soviet tanks crushed the liberal regime of reformist Imre Nagy and restored a hard-line Communist Party cabal to power, Ike also pledged his administration to continued support of the United Nations.

Khrushchev Welcomes China's Chou To Moscow

Traditional comradely bear-hugs and warm smiles were on show in Moscow today as Soviet leaders Nikolai Bulganin and Nikita Khrushchev gave fraternal greetings to Chinese delegates led by Prime Minister Chou En-lai, arriving for a summit of the world's Communist super-powers.

While Russian TV viewers and newspaper readers got the full party line of undying admiration and friendship, foreign observers had a pretty good idea that the atmosphere was less amicable behind closed doors.

The two nations continue to have severe rivalry problems - most especially in Moscow's support for Manchurian and Vietnamese communists - and a fundamental disagreement over the ways communism should be enforced. Although Khrushchev's clampdown on Hungary met with Chinese leader Mao Tse-Tung's approval.

Cancer Claims Screen Tough Guy Bogart

HUMPHREY BOGART, the Oscar-winning tough guy once told a slight lisp made his dream of stardom a non-starter, died today in his Hollywood home at the age of 56. He had lost his fight against throat cancer.

A classically educated man whose lisp was caused by an injury during a spell in the US Navy, Bogart became a comedy stage actor on Broadway before making five forgettable movies in the early thirties. In 1936 he got his first decent role, opposite Leslie Howard in *The Petrified Forest,* to prove his potential.

It was director John Huston who helped realize that potential and create the cynical good-bad guy image Bogart was to develop so superbly. The 1941 movies *High Sierra* and *The Maltese Falcon* were topped by the 1942 classic Casablanca to begin Bogart's reign as the world's favourite hard-man with soul.

In 1944, while filming *To Have And To Have Not,* he met, fell in love with and married Lauren Bacall. She was at his bedside when he died. A huge box office star, Bogart did not gain the kudos of a Best Actor Academy Award until 1951, when his performance in *The African Queen* won him that long-overdue title.

Gomulka Victorious In Polish Polls

Wladyslaw Gomulka, the Polish leader elected his country's President last October only 12 months after being released from four years 'protective custody' imposed by Soviet dictator Josef Stalin, today emerged triumphant in elections which confirmed him as all-powerful First Secretary of Poland's Communist Party.

Faced with the reality of Soviet reaction to Hungarian calls for democracy, Gomulka is tempering his aim of a specifically Polish form of socialism with continued Polish-Soviet defence links.

He has ended collective farming, however, returning four-fifths of arable land to private hands, and has curbed the worst excesses of Poland's secret police.

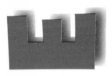

London Rocks As Haley's Comets Touch Down

LONDON GOT ITS FIRST TASTE of genuine American rock 'n' roll tonight as The Dominion Theatre played host to Bill Haley and His Comets, the band whose early international success with *Shake, Rattle And Roll* and the multi-million seller *Rock Around The Clock* in 1955 helped spark a teenage revolution. And the 3,000 audience showed just how much they liked that first taste as they danced and cheered their way through the sell-out show.

The arrival of Haley, a former country and western singer who only recorded *Rock Around The Clock* as a favour to his manager, had brought the port of Southampton to a halt yesterday as thousands of fans fought to catch a glimpse of him and his group leaving the liner Queen Elizabeth. Wild scenes also greeted his train as it pulled into London's Victoria Station.

Tonight's concert, which featured most of the hits which have given Haley combined world record sales of more than 22 miliion in only two years - including *Rockin' Through The Rye, See You Later Alligator* and the newly-released title song from his new movie *Don't Knock The Rock* - also highlighted the gymnastic abilities of Comets sax player Rudy Pompelli. He played raucous solos lying on his back and standing astride a prone bassist.

While everyone was knocked out by Haley's show and band, some expressed doubts about his long-term future. At the age of 29, plump and thin of hair, Bill Haley doesn't have the appeal of the many younger, leaner and sexier rock 'n' rollers who have followed his lead. But, for tonight at least, he was king.

BBC-TV Launch
Daily News Magazine

A new weekday news magazine hit British TV screens for the first time this evening when BBC Television launched Tonight, its soon-popular fix of current affairs and features fronted by Cliff Michelmore, one-time radio host of the forces' record request show Two-Way Family Favourites. Other regulars who'd become familiar and popular presenters included the ever-travelling Alan Whicker, Derek Hart, the irascible Scot Fyfe Robertson and a young Magnus Magnusson. Signing off became the task of folk singers Robin Hall and Jimmie MacGregor, whose own careers achieved lift-off with this daily plug of their talents.

Hungarian Uprising Leaders Go On Trial

In Budapest today, the final crushing of the Hungarian uprising was given the patina of legal respectability when the first trials began of those accused of leading or participating in the movement Russia supressed so brutally last November. Missing from the collection of intellectuals, politicians, journalists and academics who backed former Prime Minister Imre Nagy's bid to distance himself from Moscow and create a multi-party socialist state, was Nagy himself. It is now known that he spent 18 days hiding in the Yugoslav embassy in Budapest after the Soviet tanks rolled in, but was snatched as he left the building with the promise of safe conduct out of Hungary. He now faces a secret trial and will be executed in June 1958.

UK TOP 10 SINGLES

1: Garden Of Eden
- Frankie Vaughan
2: Singing The Blues
- Guy Mitchell
3: Friendly Persuasion
- Pat Boone
4: True Love
- Bing Crosby and Grace Kelly
5: Don't You Rock Me Daddy-O
- Lonnie Donegan
6: St Therese Of The Roses
- Malcolm Vaughan
7: Blueberry Hill
- Fats Domino
8: Young Love
- Tab Hunter
9: Singing The Blues
- Tommy Steele
10: Don't Forbid Me
- Pat Boone

FEBRUARY 23

Back-From-Dead Castro Wages War In Cuba

Socialist guerrilla leader Fidel Castro (pictured) proved that reports of his death last December were exaggerated when his small volunteer force renewed attacks on Cuban army detachments before retreating to the safety of a secret jungle outpost.

Castro, a former student activist once imprisoned for leading opposition to the regime of Cuban dictator Fulgencio Batista, returned to Cuba a little over a year ago after spending three years in Mexico receiving military training. Since then his ever-growing army of skilled militia and peasant recruits has harassed and disrupted police and army positions in rural areas.

On December 2, President Batista claimed that Castro and his two brothers had been killed in an airstrike on their Oriente province HQ, a claim the 29 year old has firmly proved premature.

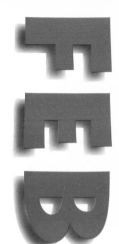

Israel Defies World Call To Leave Gaza Strip

FOLLOWING A THREE-WEEK PERIOD of mounting tension, armed clashes, riots and threats, the Israeli government of Prime Minister David Ben-Gurion today rejected a last-minute personal appeal from President Eisenhower and turned down combined US and UN demands for withdrawal of troops from the Gaza Strip and the Gulf of Aqaba.

The 70 year old Israeli leader closed the door on an immediate solution to the crisis it created last October when 30,000 tank-supported troops over-ran the Gaza coastal area between Israel and Egypt and the Sinai Peninsula in retaliation, it was said, for Egyptian attacks on land and sea communications around Gaza, and terrorist attacks from inside Sinai. That invasion was used as the pretext for the Anglo-French invasion of Egypt two days later.

Earlier this month, UN peace-keeping forces had clashed with Israeli troops in the Sinai, an engagement which fuelled the anger of the thousands of Israelis who packed the streets of Jerusalem on February 9 to protest the US-UN demands for withdrawal.

Bolstered by this display of support, and emboldened by further public reaction to the February 17 report from Cairo that Egypt's President Nasser wanted to increase pressure on Israel by keeping the Suez Canal closed, Ben-Gurion was able to tell a packed session of the Knesset, Israel's parliament, that he could not ignore the 'grave and certain danger' that Egypt would continue interfering with Israel's freedom.

Although fresh talks with the Eisenhower administration would result in a month-end statement saying Israel would withdraw from Gaza and Aqaba, the stalemate with Egypt would drag on for many years yet.

US Teens Still Think Presley's Too Much

Elvis Presley mania continues unabated in the United States where the 22 year old superstar's latest achievement is to hit No. 1 in the Billboard Hot 100 charts with his new single *Too Much* only hours after it hit the nation's music stores. The former Memphis truck driver still has two other Top 20 hits to his credit at the moment, the smoochy ballads *Love Me Tender* and *Love Me*.

Talking of smooching - some of the hottest items currently available on American cosmetic counters are a range of Presley song-inspired lipsticks. Trendy teens can now apply shades such as Heartbreak Pink and Hound Dog Orange to spice up their Saturday night back-seat wrestling contests!

More seriously - with his debut movie *Love Me Tender* a certified box-office smash, plans have been announced for Elvis to make his second screen appearance. Promised to feature more music than the first, a Civil War drama, it's to be called *Loving You*.

European Common Market Created In Rome

THE EUROPEAN COMMON MARKET, an economic alliance aimed at creating one of the world's biggest international communities, and allowing the tariff-free movement of goods, people and money across existing borders, came into being today when six countries - France, West Germany, Holland, Italy, Belgium and Luxembourg - signed The Treaty of Rome.

The founding nations foresee a united grouping of around 160 million people, although the union is to be developed in stages over 15 years. They also established a shared atomic energy programme, to be called Euratom.

A notable absentee from the official signing ceremony, which was broadcast live over the Eurovision network, was Britain. Previous British administrations decided not to get involved in the new body, preferring to lead the creation of a wider continental trading structure which would embrace Britain, the Common Market and others.

Prime Minister Harold Macmillan, who privately believes Britain should have sought Common Market membership, now has the task of selling the concept of a European Free Trade Area which, while it would include all of western Europe, would crucially involve a lesser surrender of sovereignty than EEC membership implies.

As it stands, a stand-alone Britain faces a far greater economic threat as the Common Market develops. This could cause friction rather than increased European unity, and Macmillan has made no secret of the risks Britain faces in taking this route, even if - as he has said - 'there are also great prizes' available if British industry can meet the competition the Common Market will pose.

BEA Grounds Viscount Fleet After Manchester Crash

A week after 22 people were killed and a number of houses were demolished when a British European Airways *Viscount* turbo-prop airliner crashed at Manchester's Ringway Airport, the airline today grounded all Viscounts while aviation experts determine the cause of the disaster.

Five *Viscount* flights from London were cancelled immediately, and one *en route* to Tel Aviv was stopped and grounded at Rome's Ciampino airport.

The most popular theory among experts is that a wing flap failure could have caused the crash. If only one flap extended as the *Viscount* attempted to land at Ringway, the plane would tilt over without warning - something eye-witnesses on the ground reported as happening.

UK TOP 10 SINGLES

1: Young Love
- Tab Hunter
2: Don't Forbid Me
- Pat Boone
3: Knee Deep In The Blues
- Guy Mitchell
4: Don't You Rock Me Daddy-O
- Lonnie Donegan
5: Singing The Blues
- Guy Mitchell
6: Long Tall Sally
- Little Richard
7: Garden Of Eden
- Frankie Vaughan
8: True Love
- Bing Crosby and Grace Kelly
9: Banana Boat Song
- Harry Belafonte
10: Friendly Persuasion
- Pat Boone

San Francisco Hit By Major Quake

San Francisco was tonight struggling to recover from the worst series of earth tremors to hit the area since the Great Earthquake of 1906 flattened the Californian city.

A state of emergency was imposed as firefighters and medical teams fought to rescue the hundreds of people trapped in collapsed buildings, many of which were ablaze as gas and power lines fractured under streets ripped up by the tremors.

Most dramatic visual record of the disaster was local TV film footage of the world-famous Golden Gate Bridge, which buckled and twisted alarmingly during the worst shocks.

Born this month:
8: Clive Burr, UK rock musician (Iron Maiden)
8: Marlon Jackson, US pop/soul entertainer (Jackson Five)
20: Spike Lee (Shelton Jackson Lee), revolutionary black film-maker, writer, actor (*She's Gotta Have It, Do The Right Thing, Malcolm X*, etc)
27: Billy McKenzie, UK rock musician (The Associates)

DEPARTURES

Died this month:
11: Admiral Richard Byrd, US aviation pioneer, explorer *(see Came & Went pages)*
13: John Middleton Murry, author
16: Constantin Brancusi, Rumanian sculptor
20: Charles Kay Ogden, linguist (originator of Basic English)
28: Christopher Morely, US novelist and playwright

MARCH 24

Ike And Mac Bury The Hatchet In Bermuda

THE UNITED STATES and Britain are buddies again, and that's official. A communiqué issued in Bermuda today at the end of a four-day summit between President Eisenhower and PM Harold Macmillan, proved that they have settled their Suez Canal crisis quarrel and found new areas of agreement to cement their alliance.

The summit, held at Ike's suggestion, was important if the US administration's anger at the Anglo-French invasion of Egypt last November - a needless strike the President remains certain came amid collusion between Britain, France and Israel - was to abate. With Sir Anthony Eden disgraced and retired, Ike is happy to do business with his successor, a man known to have opposed Eden's reckless adventure.

The summit statement reunited the two leaders in condemnation of Soviet repression of its Eastern Bloc neighbours, described NATO as the cornerstone of US-UK policy in the West, and welcomed the birth of the European Common Market.

Ike stressed the importance of 'the long-term bonds' which bind America and the British, proving his words by announcing a new deal for the US to supply Britain with guided missiles, with warheads controlled by American military personnel.

MARCH 6

UK Bows out of Ghana

The symbolic midnight lowering of the British Union Jack flag and the raising of a new national standard, signalled the start of countrywide celebrations which greeted the birth of Ghana, Africa's first black state, today. The Queen was represented by the Duchess of Kent. Formerly known as The Gold Coast and run as a British crown colony since 1874, Ghana's independence was welcomed in the capital, Accra, by Dr Kwame Nkrumah, its first Prime Minister and self-styled liberator of his people. The name, 'Ghana', has been adopted by Nkrumah as an inspiration for his people to recapture a time when Africans had wealth and power. It is taken from the Islamic empire which existed for hundreds of years in the Sudan during the Middle Ages.

MARCH 6

Irish Elect De Valéra President

Eamonn de Valéra, the New York-born hero veteran of the Easter Rising against the British in 1916, one-time President of the republican Sinn Féin party, founder of its principal rival Fianna Fáil and three times his country's Prime Minister, was today elected Eire's President. His 120,000 majority reflects the respect the Irish electorate has for de Valéra, who has maintained his fight for a united Ireland since a new constitution in 1937 saw the emergence of the sovereign democratic state he now heads. At the age of 75, de Valéra will continue to rail against the division of his island, though now as a relatively powerless but still influential figurehead.

MAR

Pop Fans Rush To Board Non-Stop 6.5 Special

British rock and pop fans have made BBC-TV's Saturday evening 6.5 Special one of the most outstanding instant hits in local television history. Only two weeks after its launch on February 16, the fast-moving teen show is the country's most popular. Featuring regular 'house band' Don Lang And His Frantic Five, its success has been helped by a four-week guest slot for Tommy Steele, the cockney rocker being billed as Britain's answer to Elvis Presley.

Other early guests have included skiffle king Lonnie Donegan, while hosts Pete Murray and Josephine Douglas add an irreverent laid-back style to their introductions for the likes of The King Brothers, newcomers Jim Dale, Terry Dene and the outrageous Wee Willie Harris, as well as the more established Humphrey Lyttleton Jazz Band and Tony Crombie's Rockets.

And they said it wouldn't last....!

GUINNESS AND LEAN LEAD THE WAY AS RIVER KWAI SWEEPS OSCARS

The annual Academy Awards ceremony this year turned into a triumphal procession for just about everyone who'd sweated for months in the jungles of Ceylon to make the prisoner-of-war classic *The Bridge On The River Kwai* - with the absence of nominations in the two female acting categories being due to the simple fact that it had an entirely male cast!

For the record, *Bridge On The River Kwai* ran off with no less than seven of the eight Oscars for which it was justly nominated, with Sessu Hayakawa (who played the Japanese camp commandant) losing the tussle for Best Supporting Actor to American comedian Red Buttons. Ironically, he won his deserved statuette for *Sayonara,* the movie in which Marlon Brando played a Japanese houseboy and for which the Japanese Miyoshi Umeki became the first Asian to win an Academy Award, as Best Supporting Actress!

Back to the steamy jungles. Besides winning the Best Picture prize, giving David Lean the Oscar as Best Director and Alec Guinness a prized door-stop as Best Actor, *Bridge On The River Kwai* gave both cinematographer Jack Hildyard and editor Peter Taylor the chance to give thank-you speeches, and British composer Malcolm Arnold the opportunity to omit thanking whoever wrote *Colonel Bogey,* the immortal march with rude words which formed the centrepiece of his Oscar-winning score.

The seventh win - for Adapted Screenplay - was fairly controversial, and brought the Academy once more up against the dreaded blacklist Hollywood had created to bar people who'd either admitted or been named as having socialist tendencies in the notorious Senate Un-American Activities hearings.

Although awarded to French author Pierre Boulle, it should have gone to the blacklisted Carl Foreman and Michael Wilson, because it was actually their work which translated Boulle's French-language story into a movie. It would not be until 1985 that the Academy would acknowledge them, and present Oscars to their widows.

Strangely, it would not be until 1986 that Paul Newman would win an Oscar (for *The Color Of Money*), but this year Mrs Newman - actress Joanne Woodward - took her Best Actress award home after winning it for *The Three Faces Of Eve.* In that category she faced competition from Deborah Kerr (*Heaven Knows, Mr Allison*), Anna Magnani (*Wild Is The Wind*), Elizabeth Taylor (*Raintree County*) and Lana Turner (*Peyton Place*). All in all, a pretty good year for the Oscars, for the mostly-British team who made *Bridge On The River Kwai* - and for Jimmy Van Heusen and Sammy Cahn, who won the Best Original Song award for *All The Way.* We all know just how good that sounded when Albert Francis Sinatra got hold of it.

Alec Guinness in the multi-award wining Bridge On The River Kwai

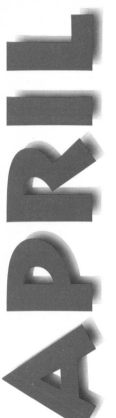

APRIL 3

Fellow Pros Vote Finney Player Of The Year

In London this evening, England's soccer professionals confirmed what Preston North End supporters have long been claiming - their dazzling centre-forward Tom Finney is Footballer of the Year.

A genuine two-footed and fearless striker, Finney has racked up a 12-year international career which has given him 76 caps and a record 30 goals, but the 35 year old's loyalty to his hometown team has meant a shortage of domestic trophies. The closest he'd come to those was losing the 1952-53 season First Division title to Arsenal on goal difference, and an FA Cup loser's medal in 1954 when Preston met a dogged West Bromwich Albion and a 3-2 defeat.

Tonight's award goes some way to setting the record straight. Tom Finney is one of the all-time greats.

APRIL 14

Courageous Hussein Defeats Jordanian Coup Attempt

KING HUSSEIN, THE 22 YEAR OLD RULER of Jordan (pictured) trying to steer his own course through the increasingly turbulent waters of Middle-East politics since breaking his close links with Britain, has displayed outstanding personal courage to quell a coup attempt by left-wing forces. At one stage he drove through heavy cross-fire to confront rebel leaders.

According to reports released today, the young King was challenged by his long-time intimate friend General Abu Nuwar, the 34 year old army Chief of Staff, who'd been won over by followers of former Prime Minister Nabulsi, sacked by Hussein five days earlier when he announced his intention to form a republic with Egyptian and Syrian backing.

Taking advantage of widespread unrest and the fact that a new government had not yet been appointed, Nuwar replaced the loyalist Armoured Regiment north of Amman with the left-wing Fourth Infantry, and cordoned off the capital.

Hussein summoned Nuwar to the royal palace and drove with him to the rebellion site. En route he stopped an attempt by loyalist troops to kill Nuwar, sending him back to the palace under guard. He then drove himself through a battle to the rebel headquarters, telling Fourth Infantry commanders: 'If I am a traitor, kill me!'

His bravery paid off and the rebels gave in. The king then returned to Amman, where he dismissed Nuwar and sent him into exile. Ten days later, as fighting continued throughout a Jordan under martial law, King Hussein appointed a clearly pro-Western government led by Ibrahim Hashem, and then flew to Riyadh for talks with King Saud of Saudi Arabia, like Hussein a strong Arab nationalist and an opponent of growing Arab socialism.

APRIL 10

Olivier Shines As Osborne's Foul-Mouthed Archie

London critics lavished praise on an outstanding *tour de force* by Laurence Olivier, who made his début at the Royal Court Theatre tonight as Archie Rice, the hard-drinking, foul-mouthed, lecherous music hall comedian in John Osborne's new play The *Entertainer*.

Olivier's portrayal of the deeply flawed and unpleasant Rice proved a revelation as he prowled the stage in a bowler hat and shabby suit to sing, rattle out a string of blue jokes and tap-dance his way to rave reviews.

The Entertainer also signals a return to the headlines for author John Osborne, whose career - and status as the original 'angry young man' - exploded in May last year when the Royal Court staged his kitchen-sink drama *Look Back In Anger*.

That play dissected British society's current ailments in brutal fashion, and critics have been quick to point out that the failure of Olivier's character to form or maintain relationships is another clever Osborne metaphor for the disintegration of British society.

APRIL 24

Mao Asks Chinese Dissidents To Disagree More

CHINESE MOVES TOWARDS reform and liberalization, launched last year by Communist supremo Mao Tse-Tung, are to continue, it was announced today in Beijing. To prove this, the Communist Party has asked government critics to explain their dissatisfactions - effectively a command from on high.

Mao's programme, characterized by his phrase: 'Let 100 flowers bloom and 100 schools argue' is his way of tackling the many problems he recognizes in Chinese society without going down the road taken by the USSR leadership in its denunciation of Stalin's reign of terror. Mao still believes in complete control, but is prepared to accept that some parts of the system could be modified.

Among the various ills identified by Mao are increased strikes caused by labour unrest,peasant and student demonstrations - which have included the stoning of Communist Party officials - and complaints from non-party government ministers who say their positions are only symbolic.

Mao's appeal for dialogue is unlikely to result in a rush of dissidents prepared to air their grievances. As long as the communists maintain an iron grip on all aspects of society, such action would be likely to incur the wrath of party officials determined to retain their positions of power, privilege and patronage.

Church Defies South Africa's Race Laws

The Anglican Church is at the heart of a nationwide civil disobedience campaign which began a new attack on the South African government's most recent apartheid laws today. At least one university board has also decided to defy rulings designed to increase areas of racial segregation.

The church campaign has the full, public and vocal support of the Right Rev Ambrose Reeve, Anglican Bishop of Johannesburg, who has told Africans to ignore the new law which bars blacks from attending churches in designated white areas without official permits. According to the church, this runs counter to the basic tenets of Christianity which say that all people are equal before God.

An equally-strong stand is being taken by Cape Town University, which is continuing to recruit and accept black students despite an edict which has reinforced educational apartheid legislation.

National Service Gets Marching Orders

Thousands of British teenagers began checking their diaries anxiously today as the government announced that National Service - the two-year compulsory military conscription of all medically-fit 18 year olds - will end in 1960.

Everyone who shared the dubious privilege of enforced service of Queen and country back then will know how important it was to those whose 18th birthdays would occur in 1960. Would they beat the cut, or face two years of bull and drill?

The decision's been made anyway. Despite protests from those who believe Britain should retain conscription to ensure sufficient manpower to meet any emergency, from 1960 the British Army, Navy and Air Force will consist of only those who want to serve.

APRIL

MAY 4

Wood Injury Destroys Manchester United's Double Bid

The young Manchester United team built by manager Matt Busby rode to London's Wembley Stadium today, quietly confident that they were on the verge of becoming the first English soccer team this century to achieve the double of League and FA Cup . They'd steamed to the League title leaving nearest rivals Tottenham Hotspur trailing eight points behind. All that stood between them and an FA Trophy were the relatively unfancied Aston Villa and 90 minutes of playing time. Six minutes into the game, disaster struck when Villa winger Peter McParland charged United's goal-keeper Ray Wood, who was carried off concussed. There was no substitute allowed back then - the Football Association remained steadfastly opposed to such 'unsportsmanlike' innovations - so full-back Jackie Blanchflower had to vacate his position and don the keeper's jersey. A 10-man United, including 19 year old Wembley debutant Bobby Charlton, were only able to limit the score-line to a still creditable 2-1 defeat.

MAY 23

Church Allows Divorcees To Take Communion

Until today, the vexed question of whether divorcees have put themselves beyond the pale and cut themselves off from the sacraments has caused confusion and controversy. That ended at the annual session of the Church of England's General Synod in London, when a vote decided that divorce no longer meant exclusion.

Conservative churchmen (and women) believed in the letter of the law as spelled out in Holy Scripture. The Bible says that marriage is for life, so divorce ought to automatically exclude the divorced from decent society, including communion. With divorce now legal in Britain, liberals thought the Church should relax that rigidity.

MAY 2

Witch-Hunter McCarthy Dies Unmourned

APART FROM CLOSE FAMILY, friends and like-minded political allies, few people mourned the death today of Joe McCarthy (pictured), the junior Senator for Wisconsin who became a major player in the American post-war anti-communist movement which found its most powerful and destructive voice in the hearings of the Senate Un-American Activities Committee.

A vocal, hyper-active and tireless self-publicizing member of the Committee, McCarthy played his part in the late forties witch-hunt conducted against Hollywood writers and actors suspected of communist affiliations or sympathies. This led directly to the creation of a blacklist by fearful studio heads and the enforced exile of many of America's most gifted creative artists as equally-frightened celebrities gave the names of 'friends' they knew or suspected of red connections or beliefs.

In 1950 McCarthy shot to prominence when he claimed to have a list of State Department officials and employees with communist links. It was a device he was to use time and again - proclaiming guilt by innuendo to create an atmosphere of paranoia without producing evidence.

Rising to chairmanship of the Committee in 1953, McCarthy's ego and arrogance took flight. When he attacked much-decorated senior military figures (again without a shred of proof) on network TV in 1954, he came up against the full weight of President Eisenhower's wrath and the belated condemnation of craven colleagues. Dismissed and discredited, McCarthy fled home to die, his damage done.

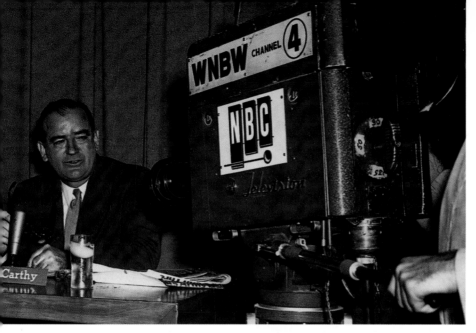

MAY 19

US Delays First Satellite Launch Plans

In Washington today, grim-faced NASA executives confirmed that US plans to launch an artificial satellite into space will not now take place in September. Although they couldn't - or wouldn't - explain the reasons for the delay, or name a specific amended date, they promised America would cross the final frontier in 1958.

There is concern in Washington that the USSR's space programme, known to be closely shadowing NASA's, could steal a lead and inflict the humiliation of second place in the space race. Apart from inflicting a hefty blow to America's international image, a Russian victory would also dent US domestic attempts to portray the communist enemy as a struggling technological backwater.

ARRIVALS

Born this month:

10: Sid Vicious (John Simon Beverly), punk rock pioneer (The Sex Pistols); Phil Mahre, US, Olympic and World slalom ski champion (27 World Cup career wins)

16: Joan Samuelson (née Benoit), US Olympic gold marathon runner

23: Therese Bazaar, British pop singer (Dollar)

27: Duncan Goodhew, British Olympic, Commonwealth and European swimming champion

DEPARTURES

Died this month:

2: Joseph McCarthy, US politician *(see main story)*

12: Erich von Stroheim, Austrian born US film director, actor *(see Came & Went pages)*

MAY 12

Five Children Among 14 Killed In Italian Race Horror

Almost two years after the Le Mans tragedy in which 83 spectators died when a Mercedes ploughed into a track-side stand, the world motor racing fraternity was stunned today when 14 people - including five children - were killed in a horrifying crash during the classic Italian Mille Miglia road race.

Italy was one of the few countries which did not apply an instant ban on road races after Le Mans. A combination of vested Italian motor interests (most notably Ferrari and Alfa Romeo) and complacency meant the Mille Miglia - run annually through rural Italy from the northern town of Brescia and taking in the

cities of Verona, Rimini, Rome, Sienna, Florence and Bologna - remained a fixture.

Today's disaster spells the end of the race. It happened when the Ferrari of Spain's Alfonse de Portago, then lying in fourth place and travelling at 170 mph (270 kph), burst a tyre and left the road. Cutting down a telegraph pole, it scythed through a group of spectators, hit a bank and careered back on to the road. Among the dead were five children, Portago and his co-driver.

The outcry, led by the Catholic Church, was immediate and overwhelming. The last Mille Miglia had been run.

MAY 6

Tunnel Link Between Britain And France?

Looking for something constructive to do with their time, now that their principal asset had been seized by President Nasser, the Suez Canal Company today revived the idea of linking Europe and Britain with a tunnel under the English Channel.

Given that the Canal Company has

an Anglo-French board of directors, the idea is being taken more seriously than most proposals this century and it's been suggested that initial exploratory work could perhaps begin at a long-abandoned Victorian site under Shakespeare's Cliff, near Dover.

There are the usual mutterings

against the idea from old buffers concerned that a tunnel could jeopardize British security and open the country to the threat of uncontrolled rabies as European animals race through the link, but the popular feeling is that benefits would far outweigh any risks, imaginary or real.

Marilyn's Hubby Convicted Of Congress Contempt

ARTHUR MILLER (pictured), the controversial American playwright whose secret marriage to screen sex symbol Marilyn Monroe became world headline news last June, was today convicted of contempt of Congress for refusing to give the notorious Senate Un-American Activities Committee a list of other writers who'd attended meetings of the American Communist Party. He now faces up to a year in prison.

A noted radical intellectual, Miller had been hauled before the Senate only weeks before he and Monroe married in White Plains, New York and left for London where she was due to start filming *The Prince And The Showgirl* with Laurence Olivier.

While he answered questions about himself fully, Miller refused to implicate any others, saying his conscience would not permit him to risk trouble for others by naming them. Advised that this stand could lay him open to a contempt conviction, the author of modern classics such as *All My Sons, View From The Bridge* and *Death Of A Salesman,* maintained his silence.

Confronted with today's judgement by a Federal court, Miller - who would spend two years fighting an eventually-successful appeal and begin work on *The Crucible,* his play about the 17th century Salem witch-hunt trials - confined his response to press enquiries to a brief: 'I have no statement to make. Neither has my wife.'

MAY

British Holidaymakers Discover Benidorm

Guaranteed sun and low prices are the principal attractions drawing an increasing number of British holidaymakers to Benidorm, the Spanish village resort, according to a travel report published in London today. Tourist development has already begun to transform the Costa del Sol community - a German company was first to build a bed and breakfast hotel there.

With continued foreign currency allowances in force, the attraction of cheap accommodation, food and drinks are pulling a growing number of Brits to Benidorm, where new hotels are going up everywhere.

The report describes most of them as 'mostly cool, spick-and-span, well-fitted...with masses of private bathrooms'. There is an added word of warning about those bathrooms, however, '..in some places, only salt water comes out of the taps'.

Eden Says His Active Political Life Is Over

Sir Anthony Eden, Britain's former Prime Minister who was forced to resign over his disastrous handling of the Suez Canal crisis and has since undergone treatment for liver disease in Boston, today announced that his active political life was over.

Although only 59 years old, Sir Anthony has been driven to his decision by continued scorn over the Suez débacle and the fact that his health really has declined dramatically in the past few months. He had three operations before becoming PM in 1955, but it is now clear that his enforced Bahamas rest at the height of the Suez crisis was not entirely a politically-motivated absence.

Eden's 21 months as Prime Minister were marked by a period of domestic prosperity but alarmingly muddled foreign policy, surprising for a man who'd been one of Britain's most able foreign ministers under Chamberlain and Churchill and was an acknowledged skilful diplomat.

While Sir Anthony would initially decline the elevation to the House of Lords traditionally the right of retiring senior ministers (even disgraced ones), he would take the title Lord Avon in 1961. He died in 1977, his reputation in no way repaired.

British Government Launches Anti-Smoking Campaign

AFTER YEARS OF SITTING on the fence, despite a succession of American and British reports linking smoking and ill-health, the UK government today announced the start of a nationwide anti-smoking campaign. It has stopped short of attempting to ban smoking in public places, however.

The government's change of heart was presented to the House of Commons by John Vaughan, Parliamentary Secretary to the Ministry of Health, only hours before publication of a special Medical Research Council report which said the link between smoking and lung cancer was 'one of direct cause and effect'.

Previous reports on both sides of the Atlantic had not gone this far, but had merely suggested an association between smoking and various bronchial and coronary ailments. As recently as 12 months ago, Health Minister Mr R Turton had rejected plans for an anti-smoking campaign, saying he was 'not convinced' that smoking caused any harm.

He may have been speaking the truth, but cynics were quick to point out that a reduction in smoking would lead to an inevitable drop in the millions the government gets annually from tobacco-related taxes.

JUNE 13

Nixon And King In Race Talks

A breakthrough of sorts for America's black community today in Washington, when Vice President Richard Nixon and the civil rights leader Dr Martin Luther King met to discuss the continuing struggle to enforce the desegregation of southern states.

High on their agenda was the continued defiance of Arkansas Governor Orval Faubus who has said he will never permit the integration of his schools and has threatened to use state militia to stop black students entering segregated establishments.

It was a meeting of vastly differing personalities – Nixon is an avowed conservative whose past includes the determined prosecution of alleged communists and liberals during his years as a lawyer, while Dr King stands for the kind of reforms and future Nixon is forced to support by by virtue of his post and Supreme Court judgments.

As long as southern state leaders continue to defy federal laws by maintaining education and electoral systems which limit black citizens' rights, the ill-matched pair will be forced to combine forces.

JUNE 19

Granada Launch Instant Hit 'Army Game'

The first networked screening of a new series is always a nerve-wracking time for everyone involved, wondering anxiously if critics and viewers will give a thumbs-up or down to months of work. The cast, writers and crew of Granada TV's new comedy series *The Army Game*, which ITV broadcast for the first time this evening, needn't have worried - they have an instant smash on their hands.

The Army Game created instant stars in the shape of the slacker Privates 'Excused Boots' Bisley (played by Alfie Bass) and 'Popeye' Popplewell (Bernard Bresslaw) and their wily Corporal Springer (Michael Medwin). Originally shown fortnightly, and broadcast live, *The Army Game* was destined to run for four years as a weekly studio production, during which time its ratings were further boosted by the arrival of the pompous CSM Claude Snudge (Bill Fraser), the nationwide adoption of Bresslaw's catch-phrase 'I only arsked', and an inevitable 1960 spin-off (*Bootsie and Snudge*) when the end of National Service signalled the closure of the Surplus Ordnance Depot at Nether Hopping.

JUNE 1

ERNIE Picks First Bond Winners

A red letter day for a few hundred Premium Bond owners today as ERNIE - the Electronic Random Number Indicator Equipment - selected its first set of winning numbers to give them tax-free cash prizes of between £10 ($30) and the top-rated £1000.

Criticized by church leaders as a 'squalid raffle' when they were introduced last year, the £1 Premium Bonds have proved a huge success with Britons - and a government which has had its national savings funds hugely increased, thanks to the carrot of a windfall win.

Body Of Missing 'Spy' Diver Crabb Washed Up

A YEAR OF RUMOUR, wild speculation and mystery surrounding the fate of Commander Lionel 'Buster' Crabb (pictured) - the Royal Navy frogman who disappeared in Portsmouth Harbour last May while the Soviet cruiser which had carried Russian leaders Nikolai Bulganin and Nikita Khrushchev to Britain for talks was moored there - reached a bizarre finale today when his headless body was found in the sea near Chichester, about 15 miles east of Portsmouth.

Although the British government was coy about Crabb's specific duties the day he vanished, it did admit he'd been carrying out trials of 'certain equipment'. It was widely assumed that he and other divers had been attempting to attach listening devices to the hulls of the Soviet cruiser Ordzhonikidze and its two escort destroyers.

That view was shared by the Russians, who were quick to have the Communist Party newspaper *Pravda* bluster accusations of 'dirty work by enemies of international co-operation' and describe the episode as 'shameful underwater espionage'.

The most popular conspiracy theories since Crabb disappeared were that he'd either been captured and taken to Moscow, or had defected - both of which today's gruesome discovery appears to have ended. In a press statement, the diver's mother insisted that her son had perished, as he'd lived, 'in the service of his own country, and of no other'.

FANGIO CLINCHES FIFTH WORLD TITLE IN NÜRBURGRING THRILLER

Juan Fangio, the Argentinian genius who'd dominated the world of Grand Prix racing to win four consecutive championships between 1953-56, entered this year's final event - the German Grand Prix at Nürburgring - needing to win if he was to achieve an unprecendented five in a row. All season he'd been hard-pressed by British newcomers Stirling Moss, Peter Collins and Mike Hawthorn, not to mention the Ferrari-Lancia Tipo 801s of Maurice Trintignant and Luigi Musso. So a German win was not guaranteed the 46 year old Maserati team leader.

What none of the thousands who packed the circuit could have known was that Fangio's victory would prove the last win of a remarkable career which he'd end after three races of the 1958 season. And they couldn't have dreamed he'd achieve his victory in so dramatic a fashion.

As ever, tactics and mathematics played equal parts in Fangio's game plan. Moss found the rough Nürburgring surface unsuitable for his Vandwall but Fangio, who had won pole position, knew that the Ferrari 801s carried enough fuel for the whole 312 miles ahead. He gambled on carrying only enough to take him 12 laps, at which point he reckoned his lighter car would be ahead enough to see him leave the pits still in the lead.

Although Hawthorn stole the lead from the start, Fangio had overtaken him by the end of the third lap and began to build up that vital lead. As planned, he came in for fuel with a 30 seconds lead. Then it all went wrong - one of the pit crew dropped a hub nut during the wheel change, and Fangio rejoined the race an impossible 45 seconds behind the Ferraris, with Collins and Hawthorn battling it out for the lead.

His car now heavier, Fangio made little progress until lap 16 when the track timekeepers had to check their clocks.

Fangio had begun hauling the British drivers in and he was now only 33 seconds behind.

Driving with all the skill and determination at his command, Fangio began a breathtaking sequence of exhibition driving during which he beat his own Nürburgring track record on 10 successive laps. He passed Collins on a corner in the last lap, and only moments later slid by Hawthorn to win by 3.6 seconds.

Carried shoulder-high through the pits by the young men he'd just thrashed, Fangio told reporters: 'I don't ever want to have to drive like that again!'

He didn't - and he wouldn't. His championship record has never been beaten.

REES LEADS BRITAIN AND IRELAND TEAM TO RYDER VICTORY

The Ryder Cup tournament between the United States and a combined Britain and Ireland team had, until this year's dramatic meeting at the Nottinghamshire course of Lindrick, been a 34-year procession of US wins, with the Brits and Irish often lucky to come second, so overwhelming was the margin of some American victories.

While there's no doubt that the loudly partisan support given the home players by the vast crowd played its part in the reversal of fortunes (and prompted one American player to say: 'Good relations? Don't make me sick!'), the simple fact is that the team led by Dai Rees played out of their skins to take the match 7-4, with one match halved.

More importantly, none of the Americans managed to win twice, the first time this had happened for 24 years.

A new pinnacle in the already illustrious career of Dai Rees, the British-Irish win was soured when Harry

Weetman, who'd partnered Max Faulkner in their 4 & 3 defeat by Ted Kroll and Jack Burke, was not picked for the singles and issued a statement saying he'd never again play in a team captained by Rees. Suspended for a year by the PGA, his sentence was reduced – at his erstwhile skipper's insistence.

124,000 SEE REAL MADRID WIN SECOND EURO-CUP

Victors in last year's inaugural European Cup Final when they beat Reims in a 4-3 thriller at the Parc des Princes in Paris, Spanish champions Real Madrid had the chance to show the full majesty of their 124,000-seater home stadium to the world - and to prove that they were still the best team in Europe - when they met Italian champs Fiorentina in this year's climax to the tournament.

With every seat sold out months earlier and the celebratory atmosphere urging them on from the starting whistle, Real stamped their authority on the game through the brilliance of captain Alfredo DiStefano and ace strikers Paco Gento and Ramond Kopa, the French star signed from Reims shortly after last year's final.

The result - a 2-0 win for Real, with DiStefano and Gento scoring - was no formality, but it was convincing. No-one could have imagined that it would be only the second of an eventual five successive triumphs for a team whose dominance is unlikely to be equalled in today's game.

INGY WHACKS 'ENRY IN FIVE

British sports writers who wrote up Henry Cooper's chances of taking the European heavyweight title from Sweden's Ingemar Johansson in Gothenburg on May 9 didn't underestimate the champion's skills, but they did take every opportunity to remind their readers that the 26 year old had shamefully - and uniquely - been ejected from his 1952 Olympic Games final against American

Jaun Fangio, driving a Maserati, leads Stirling Moss in the Argentine Grand Prix

Edward Sanders for 'not giving of his best'.

They should have remembered that Johansson, who had the added advantage of a home crowd, had exhibited his stamina and punishing punch power by taking the title a year earlier from Italy's Franco Cavicchi with a 13th round knock-out. Hardly the achievement of a man afraid of mixing it.

Johansson also had a right hand he called 'The Hammer of God'. Britain's 23 year old challenger walked into it mid-way through the fifth round and was still wondering if it was Thursday or next week when the referee finished counting him out.

It would be only two years before Johansson would become world champion by stopping Floyd Patterson in three brutal rounds. It would be six years before Cooper would get his shot at the title, when a Cassius Clay-induced cut in the fifth round ended a fight which had seen the bell saving the young champion from being counted out at the end of the fourth.

JULY 3

Soviet Army Helps Khrushchev Defeat Molotov Coup

NIKITA KHRUSHCHEV BEAT off the most serious attack on his leadership of the Soviet Union today when he won the support of the USSR's military supremo, Marshal Zhukov to ensure victory in a full session of the Communist Party's Central Committee. He has now cleared the way to remove key opponents from the ruling Politburo.

Khrushchev's defeat of the faction led by Vyacheslav Molotov, Lazar Kaganovitch and Georgi Malenkov was a close-run thing. The three - all opponents of Khrushchev's year-long de-Stalinisation campaign and seeking a return to a more rigid regime - engineered Khrushchev's initial humiliation in a special Politburo meeting vote.

Both Molotov and Malenkov were staunch Stalinists who'd been shuffled aside by Khrushchev in the period following the dictator's death in 1953. Malenkov – First Secretary of the Communist Party and Prime Minister in 1953 - was edged out of the key party post within weeks and was forced to resign his premiership in 1955, both jobs becoming Khrushchev's.

For his part, Molotov had been ousted from his foreign affairs post in 1956 when he became openly critical of Khrushchev's reconciliation with Yugoslavian leader President Tito. So there were serious scores to settle.

Enraged and alarmed, Khrushchev contacted Marshal

Left to Right: Mao-Tse Tung, Khrushchev, Bulganin, Mikoyan, Suslov, Kim Ir Sen, Shiroky and Khohgha.

Zhukov, secured his support and called an eight-day Central Committee meeting. Packing it with his own supporters, Khrushchev won the removal of Molotov, Malenkov and Kaganovitch from the Politburo after accusing them of forming an 'anti-party group'. Three other senior party officials were demoted for their part in the coup conspiracy. Within weeks Malenkov would be humiliated by his appointment as head of a hydro-electric power station in remote Kazakhstan, while Molotov would be appointed Soviet ambassador to the even more distant Mongolia. At least they kept their lives.

De Valéra Declares Emergency Clamp Down On IRA

Veteran Irish statesman Eamonn de Valéra made the toughest decision of his long political career today when he initiated a state of emergency in the Irish Republic which allowed internment without trial and enabled security forces to begin a round-up of IRA members suspected to be involved in arson attacks and shootings along the border with Northern Ireland.

No stranger to controversy through his seven previous administrations and his own personal involvement in the Irish nationalist battle for self-determination in the 1920s, de Valéra's move came after the most recent trial of known IRA guerrillas collapsed when frightened witnesses refused to testify.

As a furious row broke out in the Dáil, with Fianna Fáil members saying de Valéra should be doing more to end Irish partition, police and troops were busy putting 63 IRA men behind bars in the Curragh military base outside Dublin.

UK TOP 10 SINGLES

1: All Shook Up
- Elvis Presley
2: Gamblin' Man/Putting On The Style
- Lonnie Donegan
3: Little Darlin'
- The Diamonds
4: We Will Make Love
- Russ Hamilton
5: Around The World
- Ronnie Hilton
6: Yes Tonight Josephine
- Johnnie Ray
7: A White Sport Coat
- The King Brothers
8: When I Fall In Love
- Nat 'King' Cole
9: Around The World
- Bing Crosby
10: Butterfingers
- Tommy Steele

World Mile Record Reclaimed By UK's Ibbotson

The world's mile record returned to Britain today when Yorkshire's Derek Ibbotson took on the Olympic champion, Irishman Ron Delany, and Czechoslovakian Stanislav Jungwirth, the new world 1,500 metres record holder at London's White City Stadium.

Watched by an estimated 10 million TV audience and a capacity stadium crowd, Ibbotson chested the tape in 3 minutes, 57.2 seconds, a full eight-tenths of a second faster than the existing time set by Australian John Landy when he became the second man to break the four minute barrier three years earlier.

Ibbotson's superiority was reinforced by the fact that, while the first four over the line ran sub-four minutes, Delany was nearly 10 yards back in second and so exhausted he had to be helped from the arena. Jungwirth was third, and England's Ken Wood fourth.

JULY 20

Mac To Party Faithful: We've Never Had It So Good

BRITISH PRIME MINISTER Harold Macmillan had a rally of Conservative Party workers cheering in Bradford, Yorkshire today when he told them: 'Let us be frank about it - most of our people have never had it so good!'

That statement, destined to enter history as Macmillan's most famous (misquoted) remark, came during one of a series of speeches the PM was making in a bid to raise party morale, sagging badly after a number of poor by-election performances and continued Labour gains in council polls.

With the Treasury admitting there could be bad news for sterling before long, Macmillan has been determined to accentuate the positive aspects of six years of Conservative government.

His 'never had it so good' comment came when he told his audience to reflect and rejoice at the difference between the British standard of living now and when they took over from Labour. An abundance of goods and freedom of choice had replaced austerity, he said. Tory policies did work.

JULY 22

British Move In To Aid Sultan Of Oman

Responding to calls for help from a beleaguered Sultan of Oman, the British government today deployed troops based in nearby Aden to fight socialist rebel forces threatening to overthrow its Arab ally.

Within a week, support for the attempted revolution was said to be petering out, and the Sultan's rule was secured on August 11 when British commandos over-ran rebel headquarters in Nizwa. Within four days the UK contingent was packing to leave.

Arab nationalist distrust of the pro-Western Sultan would continue, despite the UN rejection of a joint Arab motion on August 20 condemning Britain's role in subduing the rebellion.

JULY 22

BP And Shell Quit Israel To Pacify Arabs

British petroleum giants Shell and BP today announced they are to pull out of Israel. The two have finally conceded defeat in a long and increasingly-hostile war of words with a number of Arab nations. It has become clear that their operations in those countries could be compromised - or even ended - unless they severed connections in Israel, a nation whose very existence the Arab world refuses to accept.

JULY 6

America's Althea Is Wimbledon's First Black Champ

The first black competitor to appear in the US National Championships in 1950, when she came close to beating the indomitable Louise Brough, Althea Gibson (pictured) made an even greater impact on the tennis world today when she became the first black player to win a Wimbledon title by beating fellow American Darlene Hard 6-3,6-2.

A relative veteran at the age of 30, her triumph was achieved despite appalling racial restrictions which restricted her early career and forced her to use New York public asphalt courts to hone her natural skills.

Victor at last year's French championships, she would go on to partner today's opponent in the Wimbledon Ladies' Doubles, take this year's US and Australian singles titles, and successfully defend both the US and Wimbledon singles titles in 1958.

Also a talented golfer, she would win at least one LPGA tournament after combining a professional tennis career with that as a singer and actress, and would serve as athletic commissioner for the State of New Jersey between 1975-77.

Olly, Stan's Pompous Pal, Experiences His Last Fine Mess

THE MOVIE WORLD WAS IN genuine mourning today as it learned of the death, at the age of 65, of Oliver Hardy, the corpulent, pompous half of the classic Laurel and Hardy partnership, following a stroke.

Clearly distressed, his long-time buddy co-star, the English-born Stan Laurel, told journalists: 'He was like a brother to me.'

The two transformed screen comedy through more than 200 pictures in a 30-year period. While many had slight story-lines which acted as little more than an excuse for an explosion of slapstick fall-about, the chemistry between Hardy's large, long-suffering and often exasperated character ('That's another fine mess you've gotten us into!') and Laurel's small, confused, well-meaning but inept sidekick was the template and inspiration for pretty well all comic double-acts who tried to follow in their footsteps.

Four times married and an inveterate gambler, Hardy's shaky finances and fragile ego had been boosted by the international success of recent television re-runs of classic Laurel and Hardy movies. He and Stan had also enjoyed live success as recently as 1947 when they visited Britain to appear as acclaimed guests in the Royal Variety Show.

US Trials Begin On 'Drunkometer'

Called 'The Drunkometer' and designed to measure the amount of alcohol in the breath of those ordered to blow into its nozzle, America's newest weapon in the war against drink-driving began to be used in nationwide tests today.

More than any country, America has an immense car-driving population with a corresponding number of drink-related incidents and accidents which authorities are sometimes unable to prove with existing tests. Scientists now appear to have devised a workable solution with a machine capable of being used on the spot to help confirm police suspicions.

Twenty Arrested After Ulster Booby-Trap Death

Twenty known Irish nationalists, most of them believed to be members of the IRA, were being held in Northern Ireland cells tonight following the death of an Ulster policeman in a booby-trap bomb explosion. The blast comes only weeks after Eireann leader Eamonn de Valéra's controversial introduction of a state of emergency designed to give his security forces greater freedom to hold those it suspects of IRA membership and responsibility for attacks like today's.

UK TOP 10 SINGLES

1: Love Letters In The Sand
- Pat Boone
2: All Shook Up
- Elvis Presley
3: Teddy Bear
- Elvis Presley
4: Island In The Sun
- Harry Belafonte
5: Gamblin' Man/Putting On The Style
- Lonnie Donegan
6: We Will Make Love
- Russ Hamilton
7: Little Darlin'
- The Diamonds
8: Bye Bye Love
- The Everly Brothers
9: Last Train To San Fernando
- Johnny Duncan & The Blue Grass Boys
10: Diana
- Paul Anka

ARRIVALS

Born this month:

7: Aleksandr Dityatin, USSR/RUS gymnast superstar

17: Robin Cousins, British figure skating star, Olympic gold medallist 1980, now coach and TV commentator

19: Melanie Griffith, film actress (*Paradise, Born Yesterday*), Best Actress Oscar nominee (*Working Girl*)

24: Stephen Fry, English film and TV actor, novelist, humorist (as actor: *Peter's Friends, Jeeves & Wooster, A Little Bit of Fry and Laurie;* as author: *The Liar, The Hippopotamus)*

27: Bernhard Langer, German pro golfer

DEPARTURES

Died this month:

7: Oliver Hardy, US film comedian *(see main story)*

24: Albert Sammons, British violinist

AUGUST 6

Emigration Flow Shows No Sign Of Slowing

Although Prime Minister Harold Macmillan may believe Britons have never had it so good - and full employment figures do suggest the country is enjoying a period of comfortable prosperity - the flow of people emigrating to the Commonwealth shows no sign of decreasing.

According to figures released by the government in London today, a worrying 2,000 people are still quitting Britain every week.

While most are leaving for Australia and Canada, both still offering highly attractive packages to much-needed qualified professionals and their families, there are signs that a number of valuable science and medical graduates are choosing to take up better-paid jobs in the United States - a sort of 'brain drain', if you like.

Chimes At Midnight Mark Malayan Independence

IN TIME-HONOURED TRADITION, the sound of clocks striking midnight marked the moment when Malaya - Britain's last major Asian colony - became a self-governing member of the Commonwealth, a nation in its own right.

The end of 170 years of British rule ended with the lowering of the Union Jack in Kuala Lumpur, the raising of Malaya's new flag and the undisguised delight of the thousands of Malays, Indians, Chinese, Eurasians and Europeans who represented Malay's rich cultural mix at the official ceremony.

The road to independence had been an often rocky one, Malayas premier, Tengku Abdul Rahman, reminded the crowd. He praised the Malay and British troops who'd quelled the communist guerrilla forces which had threatened the country's stability and delayed its newfound status, but warned that the scourge of terrorism remained to be obliterated and appealed to Malays to work together so people could be free to go wherever they chose, without fear.

The Chief Minister, who was elected to a five-year term of office as Malaya's first PM on August 3, was generous in his praise for the departing British. 'We were blessed with a good administration', he said, adding: 'Let this legacy left by the British not suffer in efficiency or integrity in the years to come.'

Chelsea Unleash Wunderkind Greaves

The start of a new soccer season in England, and West London's Chelsea FC amazed and excited their supporters and more objective observers with the first team début of a 17 year old forward - Jimmy Greaves.

Although relatively small and slight, Greaves immediately proved himself an instinctive goalscorer with incredible speed and inventiveness which belied his lack of years and league opponents did well to pay him the courtesy of assigning their most experienced defenders to trying to contain his brilliance. In many cases it would prove a thankless - and pointless - task.

During his club and international career, Greaves would score 44 goals in 57 national appearances (including two hauls of four goals and four of three) and notch up a remarkable trio of five-goal games in his 357 League games for Chelsea, Tottenham and West Ham. A serious drink problem forced his retirement, but he made a triumphant return to sobriety and a career as one of television's most popular sports pundits.

39

HITS AND HEADLINES: THE OUTRAGEOUS LITTLE RICHARD

No-one sang rock 'n' roll like Little Richard, and the world's teenaged record-buyers were quick to take the 24 year old to their hearts when he first exploded on the scene at the end of 1955, with *Tutti Frutti,* his debut single for the LA-based Specialty label and the immortal opening line 'Awopbopaloobopawopbamboom!' ended the relative obscurity of three years of flops and confirmed grown-ups suspicions that rock had been sent from Mars.

While *Tutti Frutti* would go on to become a rock standard - and unbelievably inspire a cover version by Pat Boone - it wasn't until April 1956 that the powerful six-foot-plus Richard Wayne Penniman would score his first major US chart hit, with the equally-distinctive *Long Tall Sally.*

This year, especially in Britain, proved that his previous exploits had merely been a warm-up for the main event. By the end of 1957, Little Richard had scored an incredible seven British Top 20 hits, with only Elvis Presley doing better. In order, they were *Long Tall Sally,* a re-released *Tutti Frutti, She's Got It,* (twice), *The Girl Can't Help It, Lucille* and *Jenny Jenny.*

His stage act, as mind-boggled concert-goers learned when he visited Britain for a sell-out tour, was the most exciting, flamboyant and outrageous thing anyone had ever seen, with the star just as likely to jump on the keys of the piano he pounded as he was to play it with his fingers. Journalists and editors loved him, and the headlines loomed thick and fast.

Little Richard made the biggest news of all at the end of the year when, during a tour of Australia, he threw his famous jewellery collection off Sydney Harbour Bridge and announced he'd decided to quit rock 'n' roll. Instead of singing the devil's music, he would return to the Seventh Day Adventist Church in which he'd spent his childhood in Macon, Georgia. He would return, of course, after a couple of years out, then retire again to found his own ministry in Los Angeles, admitting an astonishing life of bisexual promiscuity.

Result? Why, more headlines, of course!

BOY-NEXT-DOOR PAT LEADS THE SQUEAKY-CLEAN PACK

You couldn't have a greater contrast, image-wise or musically, than Little Richard and Pat Boone. While Richard represented the raunchy, real roots of rock 'n' roll, Pat Boone carried the banner of wholesome Middle America teenagery, right down to his pure white shoes, his pearl white teeth and his refusal to kiss the leading ladies in his movies.

What's more, Boone was a happily-married (with four children) 23 year old university graduate whose springboard was the influential and very nice Arthur Godfrey TV show. In 1955 and 1956 he'd bizarrely had hits with covers of Fats Domino's *Ain't That A Shame* and Little Richard's *Tutti Frutti* and *Long Tall Sally,* but it was the string of easy ballads like *Love Letters In The Sand, April Love, Remember You're Mine, Friendly Persuasion* and *Don't Forbid Me* which made him one of the world's most successful recording artists in the fifties and led to his being invited to perform at President Eisenhower's Inaugural Ball in Washington this January.

Inspiring a pack of squeaky-clean wannabes like Tab Hunter, Tommy Sands and Russ Hamilton, Boone continued to enjoy hits well into the sixties, when he began concentrating on more religious material to reflect his fervent and fundamentalist Christianity. Still performing world-wide - and still a firm favourite for women Of A Certain Age - Pat Boone was a phenomenon.

DON AND PHIL
- KEEPING IT COUNTRY

Given the importance of country music to the blend which made up the rock 'n' roll of Elvis Presley, Bill Haley, Jerry Lee Lewis and Carl Perkins, it was inevitably only a matter of time before someone would make it big performing in an almost pure country style. The Everly Brothers were the ones who did it, breaking through this year to begin an impressive ten-year reign as singers, songwriters and influential stylists.

Don (20 years old this year) and Phil (aged 18) were the sons of Ike and Margaret Everly, a successful country radio show couple who'd added the boys to their act as soon as they could hold any of the old hillbilly and gospel songs they featured on the Kentucky and Chicago stations they variously broadcast from in the 1940s and 50s.

The distinctive sound of The Everly Brothers first hit the US charts in June, when *Bye Bye Love,* one of the many compositions of husband and wife team Felice and Boudleaux Bryant the brothers would record through the years, started the ball rolling. Followed before year end

Little Richard - 'Awopbopaloobopawop bamboom'

by *Wake Up Little Susie,* they'd also score massively in Britain.

Among the other classics which would make The Everly Brothers one of the most successful acts of the decade were *All I Have To Do Is Dream* (a British No.1 for eight weeks in 1958), *Bird Dog, Problems, 'Til I Kissed You* and *Poor Jenny,* though their influence would be obvious in many of the English sixties groups who'd eventually overshadow them, most especially The Hollies.

SEPT

National Guard Enforce Little Rock School Integration

AN ANGRY CROWD OF 1,500 white demonstrators (pictured) were forced to become mere bystanders today in the Arkansas capital Little Rock as more than a thousand US armed National Guardsmen - most of them paratroopers with fixed bayonets - circled the city's Central High School to enforce the arrival of nine black students and the integration of the Arkansas education system.

The presence of Federal troops ensured a quiet and orderly, if tense, day inside the yellow brick school. Outside, seven protestors were arrested and one knocked down as he tried to grab a Guardsman's rifle when the crowd attempted to break the cordon. Their shouts of 'Go home, niggers!' confirmed there are many southern whites determined to resist enforced desegregation, or integration of any kind.

President Eisenhower's decision to send Federal troops into Arkansas, and bring the state militia of Governor Orval Faubus under federal control, has stunned many - not least those southern state governors who met at Sea Island, Georgia, this afternoon to demand the withdrawal of Federal forces 'at the earliest possible moment' and an emergency meeting with Ike.

They view the President's action as a major threat to states' rights, but the bravery of his move proves he is just as determined to ensure that Federal laws are upheld, even if it means the use of armed force.

The Little Rock action was forced on him when Governor Faubus ordered his state militia to bar the entry of all black children to Central High, saying he would never allow them to attend a white school, regardless of orders from the Federal District Court to do so, or threats of a government injunction. He argued that he was acting 'to preserve peace and prevent bloodshed'.

UK Death Toll Mounts As Asian Flu Hits

Described by a Ministry of Health spokesman as 'essentially a mild one', the Asian flu epidemic sweeping Britain is reported to have killed 39 people in the week ending September 14, while deaths from bronchitis and pneumonia have leaped dramatically during the same period.

Officials blame the added complication of chest infections for the increased death toll, saying the flu itself would not cause the number of fatalities so far reported.

A total of 160 English and Welsh towns appear to be worse affected, with reported deaths from the flu rising from eight to 47, those caused by pneumonia rising from 177 to 245, and those due to bronchitis increasing from 128 to 158. With children among those at greatest risk, a number of schools have closed as concerned parents begin keeping them at home.

UK TOP 10 SINGLES

1: Diana
- Paul Anka
2: Love Letters In The Sand
- Pat Boone
3: Last Train To San Fernando
- Johnny Duncan & The Blue Grass Boys
4: Island In The Sun
- Harry Belafonte
5: With All My Heart
- Petula Clark
6: Water Water/Handful Of Songs
- Tommy Steele
7: All Shook Up
- Elvis Presley
8: Wanderin' Eyes/I Love You So Much It Hurts
- Charlie Gracie
9: Paralysed
- Elvis Presley
10: Bye Bye Love
- The Everly Brothers

Christie's Mousetrap Celebrates 1,998 Whodunits

End-of-show celebrations were in order tonight in London when The Mousetrap, thriller queen Agatha Christie's murder mystery presented a capacity audience with its convoluted plot for the 1,998th time, and so became the longest-running play in British theatrical history.

None of the cast and crew who raised their champagne glasses at the party thrown for them by the producers could have known that The Mousetrap was still a relative youngster. It would eventually be forced to move to another West End theatre, but would continue to puzzle, intrigue and baffle audiences for close on 20 years more - and still be running as this book goes to press.

And who did do the ghastly deed? That's easy. It was.....

SEPTEMBER 6

Disarmament Talks End In Deadlock

The nuclear disarmament talks held in London over the past few weeks ended today as they'd begun, with the major East-West powers agreeing to continue disagreeing on every substantive point which could remove the threat of the world ending with a bang.

Marked by a series of proposals and plans which all of those representing the United States, the Soviet Union, Britain or France knew would be unacceptable to the other side before they were aired, the talks turned out to be little more than a series of photo opportunities for delegates, and the chance to show the other side in the worst possible light.

In brief, it was a nonsensical and expensive waste of time for all concerned, offering no prospect of the breakthrough all ordinary people of the world desperately want their leaders to make.

SEPTEMBER 23

Papa Doc Elected President Of Haiti

A dark day for Haiti, the former French slave colony in the Caribbean, as Dr François 'Papa Doc' Duvalier (pictured) won the presidential election.

Elected on the promise of ending a ruinous series of corrupt military-backed regimes which had followed the reformist government of President Estime since 1950, Duvalier would turn out to be a far worse dictator than any of his predecessors.

Creating a terror regime which mixed the perceived threat of voodoo magic and the very real threat of his brutal secret police force, the Ton Ton Macoute, Duvalier would engineer a new constitution in 1964 to enable him to become President for life.

That life ended in 1971, by which time Haitian society had entirely collapsed, and the twin scourges of poverty and disease were the legacy he left his designated heir, his son Jean-Claude - known as 'Baby Doc'.

Wolfenden Recommends Homosexual Law Reform

THE BRITISH GOVERNMENT was handed the hottest of hot potatoes today, when the long-awaited Wolfenden Report was published with its controversial message that homosexual acts between consenting adult males should no longer be a criminal offence.

The report, which is the result of three years' work by a government-appointed Committee on Homosexual Offences and Prostitution chaired by Sir John Wolfenden, the Vice-Chancellor of Reading University, is bound to cause an uproar and intense debate. Aware of this, the government has made it clear that it intends to spend several months testing public opinion before making any moves towards legislation.

One phrase likely to alarm and enrage the more conservative elements of society is the report's argument that the law should allow individual freedom of choice and action in matters of private morality, 'even if they are regarded as sinful or objectionable by some'.

Opponents to reform will say that the view that certain things are 'not the law's business' is a blueprint for anarchy which opens the way for complete licence in areas such as child abuse, even though Wolfenden identifies 'adult' as being over 21, still the British age of legal majority.

OCTOBER 22

US Servicemen Injured In Saigon

Thirteen US servicemen and five civilians were reported injured - some of them seriously - in Saigon today as communist guerrillas exploded a number of bombs.

It is the most serious incident in the South Vietnamese capital since 1954 when French forces admitted defeat in their war against North Vietnam's communist Viet Minh army and an international agreement split the Asian nation into two separately-governed states.

North Vietnam, led by one-time US ally Ho Chi Minh, has repeatedly threatened to reclaim the pro-Western south and there have been regular confrontations between communist forces and South Vietnamese army detachments in rural areas. The arrival of terrorism in Saigon, and the involvement of American servicemen, is an ominous development.

OCTOBER 4

Soviet Sputnik First To Cross The Final Frontier

THE SOVIET UNION HAS boldly gone and won the race to place a man-made satellite in orbit around the earth. Their artificial 'moon', called Sputnik-1(pictured with launch vehicle), today began circling the world at a height of 500 miles and a speed of 18,000 mph.

According to the Soviet Space Agency, Sputnik is a 22-inch diameter sphere weighing 83.6 kilograms - which makes it about six times heavier than the satellite NASA scientists plan to launch some time in 1958. It has two radio transmitters on board, with signals strong enough to have been picked up by RCA in the US, the BBC in London and a number of radio amateurs in other countries.

Among the first to extend congratulations to the Soviets was Dr Joseph Kaplan, chairman of the US National Committee for the International Geophysical Year, the 12 months of scientific celebration planned for next year and intended to be highlighted by the US satellite launch. Given that the Russians have severely dented American pride by being first to succeed, Dr Kaplan's description of the achievement as 'fantastic' was magnanimous.

There has been a noticeable silence from the Pentagon so far, a spokesman saying only that US military chiefs wanted to check details of the report before commenting. Although the Soviets have stressed the scientific research aspects of Sputnik's successful launch, and both sides have concentrated on the practical benefits to be had in such areas as communications and weather forecasting, there are also ominous military implications.

Manned space flight came a step nearer too - on October 17 Russia announced that its next satellite would have a live animal on board. The space race is well and truly on.

OCTOBER 3

Firebrand Bevan Helps Labour Retain Bomb Option

A sensational and controversial speech by left-wing firebrand Aneurin Bevan at the Labour Party conference today helped party leaders win an overwhelming mandate to retain Britain's H-bomb when they next return to government.

Bevan was heckled furiously by former hardline colleagues who'd tabled a motion which would have committed a future Labour administration to renouncing atomic weapons.

The Shadow Foreign Secretary clearly angered his one-time allies, and ceased to be darling of the left, when he thundered: 'If you carry this resolution you'll send the British Foreign Secretary naked into the conference chamber!'

OCTOBER 30

Life Peerage Plan To Revitalize House Of Lords

Confronted with the twin problems of an increasingly aged membership and the reluctance of a number of potential recipients to accept hereditary peerages, the British government today announced proposals aimed at revitalizing The House of Lords.

Legislation planned for next year will see the creation of life peerages and the abolition of centuries-old laws which bar women from the upper chamber.

UK TOP 10 SINGLES

1: Diana
- Paul Anka
2: Love Letters In The Sand
- Pat Boone
3: Tammy
- Debbie Reynolds
4: Island In The Sun
- Harry Belafonte
5: That'll Be The Day
- The Crickets
6: Last Train To San Fernando
- Johnny Duncan & The Blue Grass Boys
7: Wanderin' Eyes/I Love You So Much It Hurts
- Charlie Gracie
8: With All My Heart
- Petula Clark
9: Party
- Elvis Presley
10: Water Water/Handful Of Songs
- Tommy Steele

47

ARRIVALS

Born this month:

6: Peter Müller, Swiss downhill ski ace (World Downhill winner 1979,'80,'82)

7: Jayne Torvill, English skater (partnering Christopher Dean, won 4 world titles and 1984 Olympic gold with timeless *Bolero* routine)

8: Antonio Cabrini, Italian international football star

16: Sabine John, German pentathlon and Olympic heptathlon champion

DEPARTURES

Died this month:

24: Christian Dior, French fashion designer *(see main story)*

26: Nikos Kazantzakis, Greek author

OCTOBER 17

Inquiry Launched As Fire Shuts Down Windscale Nuclear Plant

ONE OF THE PILES WHICH make plutonium for military use was closed down permanently today as fire swept through part of Britain's Windscale atomic plant, releasing admittedly substantial amounts of radioactivity into the atmosphere and caused contaminated milk from farms around the Cumberland facility to be dumped.

As the government ordered an immediate inquiry into what later generations would learn was a far more serious environmental catastrophe than Atomic Energy Authority officials were prepared to admit at the time, it was known that local milk supplies contained up to six times the permissible level of radio-iodine.

Compounding the damage, thousands of gallons of contaminated milk were simply poured down drains which carried the poison out into the Irish Sea.

The fire started when uranium rods overheated. These lie in aluminium cans which are contained in channels within stacks of graphite blocks, and are cooled by blowing air over them. As the rods overheated, several cans burst to release radioactive material - according to AEA statements, most of it was carried out to sea by the wind and there was no direct hazard to the public. How this squares with the milk dumping is not clear.

While no-one in the plant was injured in the fire and Windscale soon returned to normal operations, the official inquiry would find that Britain's most serious atomic industry incident was caused by bad judgement, the wrong methods and faulty instruments, and the AEA would be accused of misleading the public over the true scale of the environmental damage.

The Windscale plant still operates. Today, however, it is known as Sellafield.

OCTOBER 18

Queen Visits Ike To Reinforce US-UK Links

It was the social event of the Washington year, and everyone who was anyone was present at the British Embassy tonight as Queen Elizabeth and President Eisenhower celebrated the 300th anniversary of the first British settlers' arrival in Virginia to re-confirm the 'special' relationship between the US and the United Kingdom.

The Queen's North American visit - which began in Canada, where she opened the new session of parliament in Ottawa on October 12 - has proved a triumph all the way, not least this evening. Tens of thousands packed the streets around The White House until midnight, hoping to catch a glimpse of the Queen and Prince Philip as they returned with the President and Mrs Eisenhower.

The royal party was accompanied by British Prime Minister Harold Macmillan and Foreign Secretary Selwyn Lloyd, who began summit talks with President Eisenhower on October 23.

Haute Couture King Christian Dior Dies

The fashion world lost one of its most charismatic and influential figures today when Christian Dior (pictured), the 52 year old French haute couturier, died in Italy.

A relatively late arrival to fashion design, Dior initially studied political science and music, travelled extensively and ran an art gallery. He did not begin selling his fashion sketches to Paris newspapers until 1935, but in 1942 cotton magnate Marcel Boussac offered him backing for his own couture house.

Dior's first collection, in 1947, was a triumph. Originally called 'The Carolle Line', it was immediately nicknamed 'The New Look', and its huge skirts and tight-waisted boned bodices were a revelation. Subsequent Dior trademarks included stand-up collars, coolie hats and the high-waisted 'Princess' look.

Also in the vanguard of a revival of classic menswear, Dior was awarded the Legion of Honour by the French government to recognize his revitalization of the fashion industry.

ERICH VON STROHEIM - THE MOVIE MARTINET

If Erich Von Stroheim had not existed, someone once noted, it would have been necessary to invent him. As it was, the bullet-headed, Austrian-born actor and director did exist, and his death today in Hollywood, at the age of 72, robbed the movie industry of one of its most outrageous and colourful characters.

Having been bitten by the acting bug at an early age, it was inevitable that Von Stroheim (born Hans Erich Maria Von Stroheim) would head for the infant film industry being established in America, and the still-virgin hills of Hollywood. His distinctive straight-backed, severe appearance made him a natural 'heavy', and he would appear in more than 30 films between 1918 and 1956, cast either as gangster or menacing Prussian.

Given his first directorial job in 1919, Von Stroheim spent the twenties establishing a reputation as a tyrannical, budget-breaking and unacceptably extravagant martinet - an image he cheerfully used to create his spooky, cold-fish character in the 1950 classic Sunset Boulevard. It's true to say that image was to make him unemployable as a director after 1928.

The inspiration of every boot-clad, jodhpur-wearing, close-cropped, hectoring movie director ever to feature as a character in a movie, Von Stroheim was a unique monster of his own making.

BENIAMINO GIGLI - VOICE OF THE PEOPLE

Raised in the shadows of the great Enrico Caruso, it was inevitable that Italian tenor Beniamino Gigli - who died today at the age of 67 - would spend much of his own incredibly successful career living with the burden of comparison. It was a burden he overcame to become an idol to millions of opera-lovers the world over and, more exceptionally, to millions more who wouldn't know Verdi from vermicelli but did know a wonderful voice when they heard it.

Erich Von Stroheim, Gloria Swanson and William Holden in Sunset Boulevard

Gigli's arrival in New York, where he made his starring début in 1922, came a year after Caruso's death when there was a huge vacuum to fill. Concentrating wisely on more lyrical than dramatic roles, most notably Rodolfo in *La Boheme,* the Duke of Mantua in Verdi's *Rigoletto,* and Des Grieux in both Puccini's and Massanet's *Manon,* Gigli stormed the Met for 13 years.

Recording, radio and concert tours helped spread his fame and popularity even wider, but in 1935 he left the US in protest at Depression-induced pay cuts. Persuaded back in 1939, he took on the heavier role of Radames in a new production of *Aida.* A star was re-born and a reputation, as one of the world's most inspirational performers, was restored.

MARCH 11

ADMIRAL RICHARD BYRD - THE GREAT ADVENTURER

There can be no greater guarantee of immortality than to have a place, or thing, named in your honour. Look at a map of Antarctica, find the Ross Sea, then look at the names given to some of the vast glaciers which feed the frozen waste of the Ross Ice Shelf: Scott. Shackleton. And Byrd. The man so commemorated was Rear Admiral Richard Evelyn Byrd, the American aviation pioneer and polar explorer who died today aged 69, and who earned his place in history the hard way - by being first.

Leader of a two-plane expedition to the Canadian Arctic in 1925, Byrd - accompanied by Floyd Bennett - became the first man to fly over the North Pole the following year. Three years later, with a crew of three, he led the first successful aviation crossing of Antarctica and the South Pole, having meantime successfully flown the

Atlantic - a trip which ended in a ditching in the sea off a fog-bound French coast.

Continuing his polar explorations and research before and after WWII, Byrd was the most natural, and popular, choice to head the scientific investigations of America's Deep Freeze operations in the Antarctic in the post-war period.

NOVEMBER 1

LYLE LOVETT - CHANGING THE SHAPE OF COUNTRY

Few things have changed quite as dramatically in the past 10 or so years than the sound and image of country music. Always big business, the arrival of a new breed of singers, writers and producers has helped make country reach out and grab a vastly-bigger audience than anyone dreamed possible, and close the gap between what's hip and what's hick.

A prime mover and shaker in that shift, Lyle Lovett - born today in Houston, Texas, but raised in the small farming community of Klein, a town founded by his German-born grandfather - has created his own unique voice by blending jazz, gospel and blues influences with country, using string quartets, a solo cello, big bands and black voices to colour his often-sly and humorous songs.

Many other artists have drawn on his repertoire to have hits of their own, and in 1989 the American music industry recognized his contribution by awarding him a Grammy. An occasional film actor, Lovett was secretly married to actress Julia Roberts in 1993 (a union which ended in 1995), but it is masterful albums like *Joshua Judges Ruth, I Love Everybody* and *Pontiac* for which he will be justly remembered for many years to come.

NOV

Russia Confirms Space Race Lead With A Dog Called Laika

SOVIET SPACE SCIENTISTS hammered home their early space race lead over the US today when they announced that their new satellite - successfully circling the earth while Sputnik continues its orbits - is occupied by a little dog called Laika.

The news is especially bad for Western space 'experts' who dismissed Soviet plans to include animal life in their second satellite launch as mere propaganda, or predicted it would consist of something as completely disposable and insignificant as mice.

Statistics of Laika's satellite are impressive. The whole thing weighs 493 kilos, almost six times more than Sputnik which itself is six times heavier than the USA's scheduled inaugural satellite. It is carrying equipment to measure cosmic rays and other space phenomena besides apparatus which keeps the brown and white husky mongrel supplied with food, drink and air, and monitors her condition.

According to Soviet authorities, Laika's condition is just fine, and there's no sign she's anything but content to whizz around in orbit 1,000 miles above the earth. Her response to prolonged weightlessness will give invaluable information to Russian scientists as they push on with their next big step - the successful launch of a manned satellite.

In the meantime, their plans are focused on the welcome-back party they'll throw for Laika when she returns safely to Mother Russia.

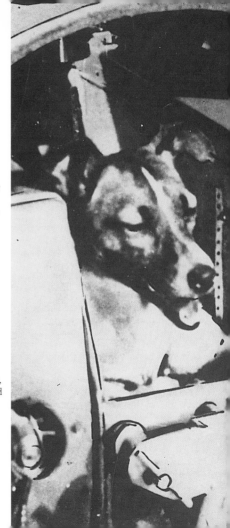

NOVEMBER 14

Socialites Mourn Queen's Abolition Of Debs' Big Moment

Britain's high society matrons were in a state of disbelieving shock today when a Buckingham Palace spokesman announced the Queen had decided that next March's traditional presentation of debutantes at Court - the highlight of the deb season - will be the last. Quite simply, she thinks has no place in the New Elizabethan era.

Presentation at Court was reserved for the daughters of the aristocracy and those prominent in society. Those who made their curtsies to the Queen were sponsored - and chaperoned - by women who had been presented themselves. It's an open secret, however, that a number of socially ambitious parents had arranged 'fee and expenses' arrangements with qualified chaperones who'd fallen on hard times, to ensure their daughters were presented. Prince Philip is believed to be the prime mover behind the decision. Whether he is or not, the presentation held at Buckingham Palace on March 18 will close a page in history.

NOVEMBER 3

Egypt Calls For Hussein's Assassination

A disturbing sign of just how far apart President Nasser and King Hussein of Jordan have grown in recent months came today when Egypt Radio - propaganda mouthpiece of the socialist dictator - called for Jordanians to assassinate their young ruler.

It's the most chilling evidence of Nasser's intention to sweep aside any opposition to his plans to create an Arab coalition which could eject all Western interests and create an oil-rich empire capable of holding the world to ransom. He also wants to form a united military machine to crush the state of Israel. King Hussein is only one of a number of obstacles to his ambition. English-educated and a graduate of the Sandhurst Military Academy, the 22 year old ruler may share Nasser's hatred of Israel, but he is obviously not prepared to see a near-communist United States of Arabia. Having successfully defeated one attempted coup, the message from Cairo is not calculated to defrost his ice-cold dislike of Nasser.

Born this month:

1: Lyle Lovett, American Grammy Award winning singer, songwriter, producer *(Joshua Judges Ruth, Pontiac, I Love Everybody albums)*, occasional actor *(see Came & Went pages)*

4: James Honeyman Scott, UK rock musician (The Pretenders)

7: Jellybean (John Benitez), US dance/soul artist, record producer

11: Tim Shaw, American Olympic super-swimmer at 200m, 400m and 1500m and member of US 1984 Olympic water polo team

14: Wolfgang Hoppe, East German, World and Olympic 2-man and 4-man bobsleigh champion

DEPARTURES

Died this month:

13: Antonin Zapotocky, Czech statesman, President 1953-57

25: Diego Rivera, Mexican painter, muralist

30: Beniamino Gigli, Italian opera tenor *(see Came & Went pages)*

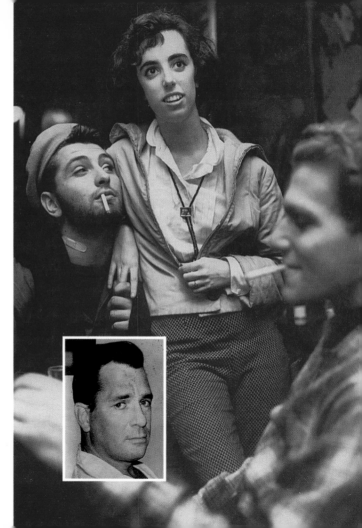

NOVEMBER 14

Anglicans Back Wolfenden Reforms

A surprise for those who thought the ultra-conservative Anglican Church would be first to condemn and obstruct the homosexual law reforms recommended in September's Wolfenden Report.

A statement released to press in London today announced that the Church of England supported Wolfenden's call for the legalization of homosexual acts between consenting adults.

The Church's decision gives a hefty boost to reformers' calls for a relaxation of the law, but as the debate continues throughout the land, the government is holding back from making a decision of its own. No-one's taking bets either way.

Kerouac's Best-Seller Reveals The Crazy World Of Beatniks

THE MOST IN-DEMAND guest on US television and radio talk shows this month is Jack Kerouac (insert picture), a French-American novelist and poet whose runaway best-selling *On The Road* offers middle America a scandalized glimpse into the fast and furious lifestyle of a generation of drinking, drugging and womanizing bohemians someone has already nicknamed 'beatniks'.

Published in September, *On The Road* has already been re-printed three times and received rave write-ups in America's most prestigious review columns. A *tour de force* description of the adventures which befall two jazz-loving hipsters as they flit between the counter-cultures of New York, San Francisco and Mexico City, the book's centre piece is an hilarious and disastrous dash from Denver to Chicago - a trip of 1,180 miles - to deliver a brand new Cadillac in a mere 17 hours!

While the 35 year old has published a number of previous books peopled by similar characters, *On The Road* has made him a media star - and he's been quick to drag a number of fellow 'beats' into the limelight with him, including poets Allen Ginsberg, Gregory Corso and Lawrence Ferlinghetti. More importantly, perhaps, Kerouac appears to have opened the way for the next generation to follow his 'what the hell?' lead.

NOVEMBER 30

Indonesia's Sukarno Escapes Grenade Attack

The Indonesian capital Jakarta was under a state of martial law tonight as security forces began hunting for associates and sympathisers of the man who hurled a grenade at President Achmad Sukarno as he drove through the city.

Dictator of the republic since 1949, the 56 year-old Sukarno has begun to succeed in his aim of uniting the scattered peoples of the Indonesian islands into a single nation, using a diluted form of Chinese communism to crush opponents.

He is still trying to rid his fledgling country of abiding Dutch interests, especially in West New Guinea. In December his call for a 24 hour boycott of Dutch businesses would be answered by an immediate ban on Indonesians trying to enter Holland. Two days later Sukarno ordered the expulsion of all Dutch nationals from Indonesia.

NOVEMBER 21

Algeria's Neighbours Plead For Peace

As the war between Arab nationalists and French forces continues remorselessly in Algeria, the divided nation's north African neighbours made their most impassioned intervention yet today. King Mohammed of Morocco and President Bourguiba of Tunisia - uneasy allies at the best of times - buried their differences at a meeting in Morocco to issue a plea to both sides in the Algerian conflict to end hostilities and begin talks.

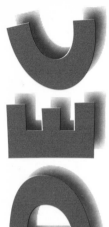

92 Die As London Trains Crash In Fog

NINETY-TWO PASSENGERS were killed and nearly 200 injured today when two trains crashed in thick fog under a rail bridge which then collapsed onto the wreckage below. The tragedy happened during the morning rush hour, in the south London district of Lewisham, when both trains were packed with City and West End-bound workers and Christmas shoppers.

Within minutes, crews from an ambulance station only 200 yards from the crash site began the grim task of locating and treating those trapped in the carnage. They were joined shortly after by Royal Engineers whose task was to try to lift more than 500 tons of concrete and steel to allow rescuers into crushed carriages.

The bridge collapse appears to have been caused when a carriage in the fast-travelling steam train from Cannon Street to the Kent coast resort of Ramsgate reared up in the collision with the back of an electric locomotive standing in Lewisham station, smashing bridge supports. Moments later, a third train - approaching the junction on the upper track - pulled up only feet from the chasm which had suddenly appeared. Fortunately, the driver had slowed because of the poor visibility, or the tragedy could have been worsened. Most of the injured were those pinned in the mass of twisted metal and concrete under the bridge - also the tomb for the majority of those killed.

British Rail believe the accident happened because the steam locomotive driver may have missed three warning lights in the bad light conditions. That must remain an uncorroborated theory, however - the driver was among those killed.

Windscale Inquiry Blames Staffing Levels

The official findings of the inquiry into October's fire and radioactivity leak at the Windscale atomic plant in Cumberland, were dismissed as a whitewash when they were announced today.

Despite overwhelming evidence that Atomic Energy Authority officials had misled the public over what happened, and what the real health dangers were, and that a mixture of bad judgement, wrong methods and faulty instruments had contributed to the disaster, today's report concluded that the whole affair was caused by 'insufficient staffing'.

While those who are against atomic power and the manufacture of plutonium have every reason to cry 'foul' and demand tougher controls over Windscale's future operations and safety measures, the verdict has been delivered and the case, as far as the government is concerned, is very firmly closed.

DECEMBER 4

UK Government Drops Wolfenden's Hot Potato

The British Government today chose to heed the results of uninformed opinion polls rather than informed, intelligent debate and announced its complete rejection of the homosexuality law reforms recommended in the Wolfenden Report.

The decision astonished and alarmed those who'd believed that the Conservatives would take the easier option of continued review, especially after the overwhelming support for reform voiced by the Church of England.

Homosexual rights protagonists would have been even unhappier if they'd known the British gay community was going to have to wait 10 long years, until June 1967 and the Sexual Offences Bill, for their calls to be answered with a law matching Wolfenden's recommendations.

DECEMBER 19

NATO Chiefs Agree To Base US Missiles In Europe

IN A MOVE GUARANTEED to do little to improve East-West relations or hasten a Cold War thaw, NATO government heads ended their first three-day summit in Paris today by announcing they had agreed that US missile bases will be set up in European member countries. This effectively means that all areas of Russia and the Warsaw Pact nations will be encircled by weapons requiring minimal flight time to reach strategic targets or population centres.

Coming, as it does, only two months after US Secretary of State John Foster Dulles offered the USSR talks on missile limitation, the NATO move could be viewed as a cynical measure designed to improve the US bargaining position if such talks should ever take place. The Soviet media choose to depict it as a clear breach of good faith and proof that US/NATO intentions are to build a first-strike capability.

While NATO officials strenuously deny this and insist the new bases are designed to improve European defences, the agreement gives Nikita Khrushchev a welcome chance to switch domestic attention away from the mounting problems of missed industrial deadlines and targets, food and clothing shortages, and focus people's minds on the greater threat of NATO's warmongering.

DECEMBER 20

Presley Fans Anxious As The King Is Drafted

Tearful nail-biting was the order of the day for millions of Elvis Presley fans as they heard that their hero had received his US Army draft papers and will be expected to report for a two-year stint of military service in March next year.

Even the hardest-nosed commentators were obviously impressed by the press statement issued by The King's manager, the ebullient 'Colonel' Tom Parker. His multi-millionaire client would, it confirmed, be proud to serve his country in whatever capacity it elected to give him, wherever it wanted him to provide that service. He wanted no special treatment or privileges.

In short, he didn't want to wriggle out of becoming just a regular GI Joe, even though some softer option probably could have been negotiated.

Behind the scenes, we now know that a whirlwind of activity was beginning as Elvis began recording enough new material to give his manager and RCA Records a two-year stockpile while his astonishing career was effectively put on hold.

DECEMBER 25

Queen Makes Xmas TV Début

Queen Elizabeth moved her annual Christmas message to country and Commonwealth into the television age today when her state-of-the-nation address was beamed into British TV sets for the first time.

One of Britain's more recent traditions, the sovereign's seasonal resumé began to be broadcast in the 1930s when it was realized that radio could be used to provide local and international subjects with a morale-boosting five minutes from Buckingham Palace.

The verdict? Although the Queen appeared a little stiff on her début, audience response was so overwhelmingly positive, she will continue to add a TV recording session to her busy official schedule in future years.

Unlike most Western horoscope systems which group astrological signs into month-long periods based on the influence of 12 constellations, the Chinese believe that those born in the same year of their calendar share common qualities, traits and weaknesses with one of 12 animals - Rat, Ox, Tiger, Rabbit, Dragon, Snake, Horse, Sheep, Monkey, Rooster, Dog or Pig.

They also allocate the general attributes of five natural elements - Earth, Fire, Metal, Water, Wood - and an overall positive or negative aspect to each sign to summarize its qualities.

If you were born between February 12, 1956 and January 30, 1957, you are a Monkey. As this book is devoted to the events of 1957, let's take a look at the sign which governs those born between January 31 that year and February 17, 1958 - The Year of The Rooster:

THE ROOSTER
JANUARY 31, 1957 - FEBRUARY 17, 1958
ELEMENT: FIRE   ASPECT: (-)

Strong-minded and extrovert, Roosters are flamboyant people who are generally self-confident. They have powerful personalities, are very determined and assertive, and although it is a very feminine sign, the Rooster is likely to be bossy and dominant - most intimidating at times!

Roosters are highly organized and won't accept any untidiness - they're happiest in an organized environment, but are very carefree when making a decision or coming to a conclusion.

Although flashy in most areas of their lives, Roosters are most prudent when it comes to managing their finances, enjoying watching money grow. They have a strong sense of business, which is well served by an abundance of stamina, even if Roosters don't always allow much weight to settle on their own shoulders and can't always deliver promised goods.

Roosters have a compulsion for winning. They need to feel they're the best, are not happy until they gain advantage over others and always want to have the last word in an argument.

Roosters' most negative aspects lie in their selfishness and sense of grandeur - they can be vain and pretentious, with a strong egotistical need to be the constant centre of attention. This can, however, make them excellent, entertaining and often funny companions in public. The down side of that is their tendency to be outspoken and frank, and rather tactless, blunt and abrasive.

Roosters have a certain duality to their character. On the one hand they're conservative and very traditionalist. On the other, they're theatrical and dramatic, seeing the world as either black or white. And, when it comes to people, they love or hate them on sight.

Because of their scrupulous honesty, Roosters are unlikely to deceive or cheat on people they decide are close or dear to them.

Roosters can be stuck-up and conformist, and are not the most compassionate people. Although extremely competitive, they prefer contests to be one-on-one. They need to shine individually in the limelight, and while their egocentricity and pride can be quite hard to take, their honesty and openness makes them fascinating people to be around.

FAMOUS ROOSTERS

HRH Prince Philip
The Duke of Edinburgh
Dirk Bogarde
actor, author
Michael Caine
actor, restaurateur
Steffi Graff
tennis superstar
Michael Heseltine
politician, businessman

Katharine Hepburn
actress
Mary Quant
fashion designer, businesswoman
Peter Ustinov
actor, raconteur, art expert
Lyle Lovett
singer, songwriter, producer, actor